PAPERBACK PLUS Teacher's Resource

Monday Run Day
Nick Sharratt

PAPERBACK **PLUS**
In the same book.
Read a poem about a week of
wild weather, and explore
a newspaper weather
report.

Monday Run Day

Every day is different for the little dog in *Monday Run Day*. Monday is a day to run, Tuesday is snooze day, Wednesday is friends day, and so on. Readers learn the days of the week and predict the rhyming words as they follow the little dog's antics.

Monday Run Day

- The selection includes author/illustrator information to share with the children.

- Colorful illustrations bring the dog and its friends to life. Children will sense that each day is a fun day for this little dog!

- Rhyming text—which includes playful, invented words—will make learning the days of the week a reading game.

- Readers will identify with the dog and its scrapes and adventures.

A Weather Map (page 28)

- A map with weather symbols and questions shows different conditions across the United States.

PAPERBACK PLUS

A Week of Weather (page 20)

- This poem by Lee Bennett Hopkins matches different kinds of weather to the days of the week. Children can read about Monday/Muggy-day, Tuesday/Tornado-day, and so on. Large colorful photos bring weather words to life.

The Five-Day Forecast (page 27)

- Appealing graphics from a newspaper help children read this extended forecast.

Choices for Reading

Reading Options

Depending on children's needs and interests, choose one of the following options for the whole book, or alternate options to read the book in segments. For all options, use the Discussion Questions on page 5, or children's own questions about the book, to establish a purpose for reading.

Reading Aloud

Choose one of these options for reading aloud:

Option 1: Read the entire book aloud. Model reading strategies by stopping to share your thoughts about the text.

Option 2: Read the whole book aloud without stopping. Then reread it using the Exploring the Book sections, starting on page 6.

Option 3: Read the book aloud using option 1 or 2, and have children follow along in their own books.

Guided Reading

Have children read the book in segments, as a class or in groups. After each segment, use the Discussion Questions or children's own questions to talk about what they have read.

Cooperative Reading

Have children read the whole book in pairs or in small groups, helping each other with the text.

Independent Reading

Assign the book, and have children read it independently.

Reading Strategies

One or more of the following strategies are recommended for each segment of the book: Predict/Infer, Self-Question, Monitor, Evaluate, Summarize. Depending on children's needs and the focus of your lessons, you may choose to follow these recommendations, to use a different strategy, or to use all the strategies.

Choices for Assessment

Informal Assessment

The Paperback Plus Teacher's Resource provides opportunities for both student self-assessment and informal assessment by the teacher. Ongoing self-assessment offers children a chance to reflect on and evaluate their thinking about what they have read. Student discussions give you many opportunities to observe and assess children's progress. The Informal Assessment Checklist on page 16 can be used during student/teacher conferences.

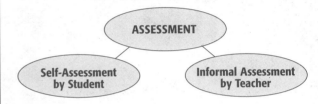

Activities

You can use the responding and cross-curricular activities to assess children's ability to understand and apply what they have read. Children can work independently or in small groups to complete the activities. You may wish to assign particular activities or to copy and distribute these pages for children to choose from.

Activity Masters

You can use these blackline masters as minilessons or as tools for assessing comprehension and critical-thinking skills and strategies.

 # Portfolio Opportunities

The portfolio icon indicates portfolio opportunities throughout the Paperback Plus Teacher's Resource.

Setting the Stage

BOOK SUMMARY

A little dog has an adventure with a different animal each day of the week. Monday is *run day*, as the title says, but Tuesday is *snooze day*. On Wednesday the dog and a buddy have *friends day*, but Thursday finds the dog growling at a cat for *grrrs day*. The patterns of rhyming words and contrasting activities continue as the animals dress up on *tie day* and play in the mud on *splatter day*. Finally, all share a picnic on Sunday—that's *bun day*, of course!

INTRODUCING THE THEME

Focus Theme:
Off to School We Go — See What We Know!

Other Themes:
Rhyme Time
What We Do
Pets

Invite children to share some of the things they learned *before* they were first graders. You might prompt them by asking volunteers to count some objects in the classroom or to identify their favorite colors; point out that they have learned numbers and color names.

Tell children that during this theme they will be reading more about many topics that are already familiar to them, such as colors, numbers, rhyming words, the alphabet, and the days of the week.

Begin a bar graph on chart paper to help children focus on some of their accomplishments. List entries such as the ones shown here, and ask volunteers to suggest others. Children can write their names on squares of construction paper and post one next to each thing they have learned. During the year, children can add squares as they learn new things.

Count to 30	Sue	Joe	Kim		
Make rhyming words	Ben				
Tie shoes	Joe	Ben	Lee	Sue	Kim
Zip a jacket	Kim	Joe			
Say the alphabet	Lee	Sue	Ben	Joe	

BUILDING BACKGROUND

Display a calendar and help children name the days of the week. Explain that they will be reading those words in the next selection.

PAPERBACK PLUS You might want to share "The Five-Day Forecast" on page 27 to introduce the days of the week. Ask children to figure out on what day of the week this forecast appeared in the newspaper. *(Monday)* Have children use the symbols to tell the weather prediction for each day that week.

Have partners practice saying the days of the week together as a chant. Then invite them to suggest new ways to say the chant; partners might name alternate days, for example, or one child might say the first part of each word while the partner responds with "day."

Ask children to name some things they do every day, such as get dressed or eat lunch. Then discuss how every day is different. Children may conclude that people do different things depending on the weather, special occasions, work or school schedules, feelings, or what their friends want to do.

Duplicate a one-week calendar. Suggest that children draw pictures to show what they like best about each day.

INTRODUCING THE BOOK

Share the book with children, identifying the title and the author-illustrator's name. Invite them to tell about the art on the cover. Here are some other ideas to spark their interest:

- Ask children about the unusual title and what they think it means. Then have them close their eyes, listen as you say the title, and tell what parts of it sound alike. Encourage them to think of other words that rhyme with *run* and suggest that they look for those words when they read the book.

- Share the information about the author-illustrator found at the beginning of the book. Point out that Nick Sharratt wrote the words and drew the pictures. After reading the information, have children explain why sunny days are important to Mr. Sharratt.

- Take a picture walk through the book. Ask children if they think they will be reading about real or make-believe dogs. How can they tell? What clues do the pictures give?

- Let children use their journals to record their thoughts, questions, or drawings about the days of the week. They can add personal responses to the selection after they read and discuss it.

CHOICES FOR READING

Exploring the Whole Book

- Invite children to think of different things a dog might do for fun. The questions below can be used to set purposes for reading or as discussion prompts after children read the whole book.

Exploring the Book in Segments

For children who would benefit from reading the story in sections, you might pause for discussion at these points:

Segment 1: Monday and Tuesday, *pages 2–5*

Segment 2: Wednesday and Thursday, *pages 6–9*

Segment 3: Friday, Saturday, and Sunday, *pages 10–19*

Discussion Questions

1. Where do you like to go when you go out to play? What do you like to do? Does the dog in the story like any of the same things? *(Personal Response; Compare and Contrast)*

2. Is this a story about real dogs or make-believe dogs? What clues helped you decide? *(Fantasy and Realism; Noting Details)*

3. What other days besides a "run day" do you think a dog might enjoy? Can you think of some that rhyme with *Monday*? *(Language Patterns)*

4. What makes the little dog smile? What makes it growl? *(Cause and Effect)*

5. Do you think the little dog has a favorite day of the week? What makes you think so? *(Inferences: Drawing Conclusions)*

Segment 1 Summary:
pages 2–5

- On Monday, the dog runs with a larger friend. On Tuesday, however, the little dog snoozes.

Developing Vocabulary

Write *Days of the Week* at the center of a word web as shown, and list each day in a circle connected to it. Then call attention to the book title. Write *run day* below *Monday,* and review how the words in the circle are alike. *(Run rhymes with the first part of Monday, and both entries end with day.)*

Encourage children to think of other phrases with the same rhyming pattern and list them under *run day*. Continue with the other days of the week. As children read the story, they can note whether the author used any of the same ideas.

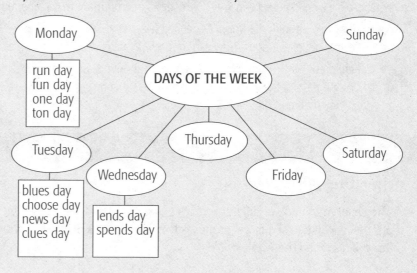

Reading Strategies

Predict/Infer Before reading, call attention to the words children listed in the web under *Monday* and *Tuesday*. Then ask children to predict what the dog will do on the first two days of the week and think of questions they want to answer as they read the story. Record their ideas. If necessary, use these prompts: Where will the dog go? Does it have friends? Who are they? What will they do together?

Discussion Questions

1. What does the dog do on Monday? Who joins in? *(Noting Details)*
2. Why do you think the dog snoozes on Tuesday? *(Cause and Effect)*
3. Name some other words that mean nearly the same as *snoozes. (sleeps, rests, naps)* Why do you think the author chose *snoozes? (Language Patterns)*
4. What do you think the other dog is doing on Tuesday? *(Inferences: Drawing Conclusions)*

Assessment

- Invite children to talk about rhyming words and any other patterns (days of the week, opposite activities) they see in the book so far. Note whether children understand the concept of rhymes and how they work in the story.

- Note how children choose and complete the activities on page 7.

- Children can do Activity Master 1: Run, Dog, Run! *(Noting Details)* on page 13.

ACTIVITIES

Choose one or more of these activities
to do by yourself or with a friend.

Social Studies: Pet Care

How would you take care of the dog in the story? Make a plan for each day.

Day	Jobs	Ways to Play
Monday		
Tuesday		

Language Arts: Rhyme Time

Make up words that rhyme with *Monday* and *Tuesday*. Draw pictures of the dog on those days and add labels.

Language Arts: A Dog Story

Write a story about the dog and its big friend. Where will they run to? What else will they do for fun?

Science: All About Dogs

Give a talk about your favorite dog. Tell these things: What does it look like? What makes it special? Why is it your favorite?

Segment 2 Summary:
pages 6–9

- Wednesday is friends day, and the little dog spends the day with another dog.
- But Thursday is *grrrs* day because the little dog growls at a cat in a tree.

Assessment

- Observe whether children relate their prior knowledge about dogs and cats to the text as they answer questions.
- Note how children choose and complete the activities on page 9.
- Children can complete Activity Master 2: That's What Happens *(Cause and Effect)* on page 14.

CHOICES FOR INSTRUCTION

Developing Vocabulary

Write the words *Monday, Tuesday, Wednesday, Thursday* on separate index cards. Have children read the words in random order. Then invite partners to practice arranging the cards in the order of the days of the week. Children can use a calendar to check their work.

Reading Strategies

Predict/Infer   Ask children what days they think will come next in the story. Then explore the artwork on pages 6–7 and ask children what clues it gives about the dog's next adventure. Write their suggestions on chart paper.

Summarize, Evaluate   Invite children to summarize what they have read so far. Then, as they read the next segment, ask them to think about the words and pictures that Nick Sharratt used. Has he made an interesting book? Is it funny? Does it make the reader want to keep going?

After they read, have children share their answers and give their reasons.

Discussion Questions

1. Who is the little dog's friend? *(Noting Details)*
2. What do you think the two friends like to do together? *(Inferences: Drawing Conclusions)*
3. Why do you think the cat is in the tree? *(Cause and Effect)*
4. Are the cat and the dog friends? How do you know? *(Inferences: Drawing Conclusions)*
5. First we read about *run day* and *snooze day.* How are those activities connected? How would you compare *friends day* and *grrrs day*? *(Compare and Contrast)*

ACTIVITIES

Choose one or more of these activities
to do by yourself or with a friend.

Comparing: What Did We Do?

Think about what the little dog did. What did *you* do on those days last week? Did you do any of the same things? Tell a friend.

Language Arts: A Friendship Tale

Will the dog and cat ever be friends? Make up a story about them. Tell how they become best friends. You can write or draw your story.

Social Studies: Dogs That Help

Some dogs help people. Make a list or draw some pictures to show what dogs do to help. Share your list with a friend.

Science: Animal Friends

Some animals are friends and some are not. Often, cats and dogs are not friends. Tell about another animal that is NOT friends with a cat or dog.

Segment 3 Summary:
pages 10–19

- The dog's antics become zanier as Friday becomes tie day, a day for wearing a tie. Saturday, the dog and friend do the opposite of dressing up: They splash in the mud. On Sunday, the dogs are cleaned up again for a picnic of buns.

Assessment

- Listen as children summarize or retell the story. Note whether they mention events in the correct sequence.

- Note how children choose and complete the activities on pages 11–12.

- Children can complete Activity Master 3: Fun Days! *(Inferences: Drawing Conclusions)* on page 15.

Developing Vocabulary

Write *tie* in three columns on the board or on chart paper, and explain that this word is in the story. Have children discuss different meanings for *tie* and think about how the author might use it. Record their ideas in the columns, using phrases or simple pictures. Discussion prompts: Will the dog tie his shoes? Will the owner tie the dog next to its doghouse? Will two dogs play a game that ends in a tie?

As children read the rest of the story, have them note whether the author uses any of the meanings on the list.

Reading Strategies

Summarize, Predict/Infer If children have not yet done so, suggest that they make notes in their journals to help them remember what the little dog did each day. They might write key words or draw a picture for each event.

Have children retell the story to this point by naming what the dog has done on each day of the week. Point out that they can *summarize* the story, or tell it in a shorter way, by thinking of a sentence that tells about all the events so far. Suggest this summary, and have volunteers propose others: *Each day the dog does something whose name rhymes with the day's name.* Then invite children to predict what will happen next.

 After children read the story, you might want to share "A Week of Weather" on pages 20–26. Children will enjoy discussing the dramatic photos and comparing the text with *Monday Run Day.* Suggest that they try summarizing in one sentence what happens in the poem.

Discussion Questions

1. How are the activities for Friday and Saturday different? *(Compare and Contrast)*

2. Who are the dog's playmates on Friday and Saturday? *(Noting Details)*

3. Why do you think the dogs are not covered with mud at the picnic on Sunday? *(Inferences: Drawing Conclusions)*

4. Who is on the last page? Why do you think all those animals are there? *(Inferences: Drawing Conclusions)*

 Together, reread "A Week of Weather" on pages 20–26. Ask children if they think the girl on page 26 and the little dog in *Monday Run Day* felt the same way about Sunday. Then invite children to read "A Weather Map" on page 28. Can they find their own state? What was the weather there the day the map was made?

WRAP-UP ACTIVITIES

After reading the book, choose one or more of
these activities to do by yourself or with a friend.

Language Arts: What Day Is It?

Think about the story. Make up some riddles like this one. Then see if a friend can answer them.

I wear a tie today.
What day is it?

Art: Tie Day

Draw your favorite tie. Make it big enough to wear. Then cut it out and wear it on Friday Tie Day!

Splatter Art

Make a splatter day painting. But use paint, not mud!

Dip an old brush in paint. Rub the brush with a stick to splatter paint on art paper. Then try a new color.

Math: Counting

Look at page 15. How many buns are on the plate? Are there enough for your class? Figure out how many more you would need and tell a friend how you did it.

PAPERBACK PLUS ACTIVITIES

Choose one or more of these activities
to do by yourself or with a friend.

A Week of Weather
(pages 20–26)
Health

Weather Clothes

People wear clothes to match the weather. Draw pictures to show three kinds of weather. Show what you would wear. Explain your choices to a friend.

A Weather Map
(page 28)
Viewing

Weather Symbols

Copy the weather symbols on art paper, or make up your own. Add a symbol for the wind. Tape a symbol on the calendar each day to show the weather.

A Week of Weather
(pages 20–26)
Science

A Weather Report

Each day, write down the weather. At the end of one week, give a weather report.

The Five-Day Forecast
(page 27)
Math

Things in Fives

With a friend, think of things that come in fives. Make a list or draw pictures. How long can you make the list?

Run, Dog, Run!

Name _____

✏️ Help the dog find its way from run day to snooze day. Draw a line from the dog to the dog's bed.

That's What Happens

Name _____

 Look at the pictures. Will the dog cause more trouble? Draw what the cat will do.

  3

✎ Write a sentence about your picture.

_____

- -

_____

Fun Days!

Name _____

✏️ **Match the days. Listen for the rhymes!**

Monday	tie day
Tuesday	splatter day
Wednesday	run day
Thursday	snooze day
Friday	bun day
Saturday	friends day
Sunday	grrrs day

🖍️ **Draw what you do on your favorite day.**

Reflecting/Self-Assessment

Make copies of the diagram below, and distribute them to children. Have them reflect on their experiences with reading the book and doing the activities.

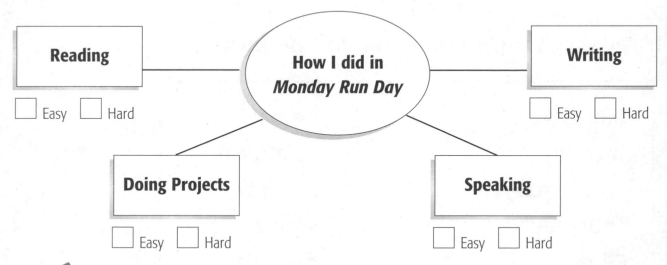

INFORMAL ASSESSMENT CHECKLIST

Invite children to answer the following questions during conference time, or observe their performance levels in using the skills listed below.

Skill	Question/Activity	Beginning	Developing	Proficient
Predict/Infer	Ask how children predicted what would happen next in the story. Clues to note: prior knowledge (animals); language patterns (days of the week, rhymes, opposite activities).			
Noting Details	Ask children whether details in the pictures helped make the story funny. Ask if the art helped them read any words.			
Inferences: Drawing Conclusions	Ask children to name something they know about the dog after reading the story. Ask if "grrrs day" was a good name for Thursday and why.			
Language Patterns	Invite children to choose one day of the week and invent a new rhyming name for it. Observe whether their responses rhyme and end with *day*.			

Bibliography

Today Is Monday
by Eric Carle
Philomel 1993 (32p)
A favorite song introduces
readers to the days of the week.

Jesse Bear, What Will You Wear?
by Nancy White Carlstrom
Macmillan 1986 (32p)
also paper
Rhyming verse follows Jesse
Bear through his day.

Three Two One Day
by Debbie Driscoll
Simon 1994 (32p)
A small girl's daily activities are
outlined in rhyming text.

Come Out and Play, Little Mouse
by Robert Kraus
Mulberry paper 1995
A cat tries to tempt Little Mouse
to come out and play.

My Brown Bear Barney in Trouble
by Dorothy Butler
Greenwillow 1993 (32p)
A girl and her bear have a
busy week filled with fun
and mischief.

Cookie's Week
by Cindy Ward
Putnam 1988 (24p) also paper
Cookie the cat gets into trouble
each day of the week.

What Will the Weather Be Like Today?
by Paul Rogers
Greenwillow 1990 (32p)
Rhyming text describes the
ideal climate for animals all
over the world.

Go, Dog, Go
by P. D. Eastman
Random 1961 (48p) also paper
The antics of many different
dogs are described in simple
text.

INVITATIONS
TO LITERACY

Houghton Mifflin

ISBN 0-395-75156-X

9 780395 751565

1-3538